FISHING

LISA KLOBUCHAR

Heinemann
LIBRARY

www.heinemann.co.uk/library
Visit our website to find out more information about Heinemann Library books.

To order:
☎ Phone 44 (0) 1865 888066
📄 Send a fax to 44 (0) 1865 314091
💻 Visit the Heinemann Bookshop at www.heinemann.co.uk/library to browse our catalogue and order online.

First published in Great Britain by Heinemann Library, Halley Court, Jordan Hill, Oxford OX2 8EJ, part of Harcourt Education. Heinemann is a registered trademark of Harcourt Education Ltd.

Editorial: Adam Miller and Kathy Peltan
Design: Joanna Turner
Illustration: Jeff Edwards and Barry Atkinson
Picture Research: Jill Birschbach
Production: Camilla Smith

Originated by Ambassador Litho Ltd.
Printed China by WKT Company Ltd

The paper used to print this book comes from sustainable resources

ISBN 0 431 11051 4
09 08 07 06 05
10 9 8 7 6 5 4 3 2 1

British Library Cataloguing in Publication Data
Klobuchar, Lisa
   Fishing. – (Get Going! Hobbies)
   799.1

A full catalogue record for this book is available from the British Library.

Acknowledgements
The Publishers would like to thank the following for permission to reproduce photographs: p. 4 George Shelley/Corbis; pp. 5, 8, 9b, 12, 13, 14, 15, 16, 17, 20, 21b, 23, 24 Dale Spartas Photo; p. 6t The Art Archive/Picture Desk; p. 6b The Granger Collection, New York; p. 7 Richard Hamilton Smith; p. 9t Doug Stamm/ Stammphoto; p. 11 Lawrence Manning/Corbis; p. 18 Steve Maslowski/Visuals Unlimited; p. 21t Ariel Skelley/Corbis; pp. 22t, 22b Bob Swan; p. 26t Kevin Fleming/Corbis; p. 26b Hooked on Fishing International; p. 28 Dinodia; p. 29 Reuters NewMedia Inc./Corbis.

Cover photograph of people fishing by Dale Spartas Photo.

The Publishers would like to thank experienced fishermen, Bob Swan, and Sam Detrent for their comments that were used to complete this book.

CONTENTS

Some words are shown in bold, **like this.** You can find out what they mean by looking in the glossary.

Part of the fun of fishing is the mystery. As your line disappears into the water, you try to imagine what is going on under the surface. Is your hook and bait just dangling unnoticed in deep water? Or is a hungry fish eyeing it, getting ready to snap it up?

Suddenly you feel a little tug on the line. Could this be a fish? You feel another tug. This time there is no doubt – you have a bite. Now you have to make a split-second decision. Does the fish have the hook in its mouth, or is it just testing? If you pull back on the rod too soon or too late, the fish will escape.

REELING IN YOUR CATCH

If you have some experience with fishing, you will know just what to do. With perfect timing, you jerk up the tip of your rod. The tugging on your line tells you that you have hooked your fish. Not too quickly and not too slowly, you reel in your catch.

Sometimes, you have to fight to bring in a big one!

ANGLING

The sport of fishing with a hook, line, and rod is called angling. The word comes from an old English word meaning "hook". People fish in lakes, streams, rivers, ponds, reservoirs, and oceans. In this book you will learn all about the sport of freshwater angling.

Fishing can be fun for people of all ages. This girl holds a big rainbow trout that she has caught.

IS FISHING CRUEL?

For many anglers, their enjoyment of the sport depends on their belief that hooking fish does not cause the fish pain. A scientific study in the USA in 2003 also suggested that this was true. The study found that fish brains do not have the necessary regions to allow the fish to experience pain. However, another study in the UK seemed to show that fish do feel pain. It showed that when irritating substances were put on the skin of a fish, the fish behaved as if it was uncomfortable. People who want to discourage others from fishing point to this new research as proof that hooking a fish through the mouth with a sharp hook is cruel.

Humans have been fishing for tens of thousands of years. **Archaeologists** have found evidence that people in southern Africa knew how to fish as early as 100,000 years ago. People back then probably speared fish to catch them. The oldest known fish hooks were found in eastern Europe. They date from about 20,000 years ago and are made of horn, bone, and wood. All over the world, archaeologists have found ancient remains of hooks, spear tips, fishnets, and weights used in fishing.

The earliest record of people fishing as a pastime is from ancient Greece. The Greek poet Theocritus, who lived in about 280 BC, wrote the first known description of fishing with a pole and line. At about the same time, the Chinese were using silk line and metal hooks to pull in fish for fun.

FIRST BOOK ABOUT FISHING

The first surviving full-length book on fishing for sport is *The Treatyse of Fysshynge Wyth an Angle*, published in 1496. That title in today's English would be *The Theory of Fishing with an Angle*.

This Egyptian artwork showing two fishermen in a boat is more than 4000 years old.

Historians believe that its author was a nun named Dame Juliana Berners. She wrote that anglers should fish with a spirit of love and respect for nature in mind. She encouraged anglers to make all their own equipment and gave readers instructions on how to do it.

This drawing of a fisherman was used in a book in 1496.

FISHING AS A HOBBY

The development of manufacturing in the mid-1800s gave many people an opportunity to experience angling as a hobby. New types of rods were developed, and the first reliable reel was invented. The first spinning reels became available in the early 1900s. In the 1930s and 1940s, **synthetic** lines and **fibreglass** rods were invented. Fishing equipment was improved both in variety and quality in the second half of the 1900s. New kinds of materials made rods stronger and more sensitive. Anglers today use electronic devices to determine water depth and to "see" what is under the water. Some even use satellite technology to find and mark good fishing spots.

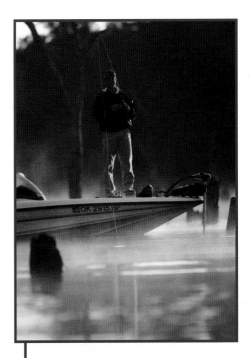

This type of fishing boat is used to fish especially for pike.

Today, angling is more popular than ever, with millions of freshwater anglers around the world. This sport is enjoyed by both adults and children.

FISH LINGO

Here are a few popular fishing expressions and their meanings:

backlash tangle of fishing line that results from a bad cast

bird's nest big mass of fishing line that is really hard to untangle

brace a pair of fish, usually referring to salmon or trout

peg location on the bankside marked out for match fishing – usually numbered

run when a fish takes the bait, sometimes at great speed

strike sharp pull on the line to set the hook in the fish's mouth.

The most basic fishing equipment is the rod and reel. Today's rods are made of various materials such as **fibreglass** and **graphite.** Some rods are long, and others are short. Some bend very easily, while others are stiff. Anglers also have several different types of reels to choose from. Anglers use different rod and reel **rigs** depending on what kind of fishing they are doing. To fish for small fish, such as roach and gudgeon, it is best to use a lightweight reel and a rod that bends easily. **Landing** a 7-kilogram (15-pound) fish usually requires a longer, stiffer rod and a sturdy reel.

The photo below shows some of the parts of fishing rods and reels.

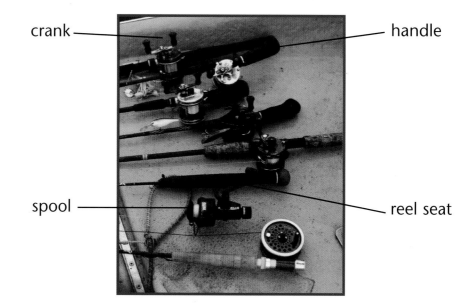

crank — handle

spool — reel seat

FOUR MAIN TYPES OF REELS

All reels have a spool for holding a line and some kind of crank for **retrieving** a **lure,** or bait. A *closed-face reel* is the easiest kind of reel for beginners to use. The spool that holds the line is enclosed in a case. The angler can cast easily without tangling the line.

A *spinning reel* has an open spool with a thin, metal loop called a **bail arm**. An angler flips the bail arm over to cast or to let out some line. Spinning reels are the most popular because they are easy to use. They also can be used to fish for all types and sizes of fish in almost all conditions.

A *multiplyer* is designed to be used with heavier rods, lines, and bait. Anglers use multiplyers when they are fishing for big pike.

A *fly reel* is simpler than other types of reels. It looks a bit like a flattened spool. Fly reels are used only to store line between casts. They are not used to retrieve the lure. Instead, a fly fisher retrieves the lure, and lands the fish, by pulling directly on the line. It is used for all sizes of fish.

This photo shows the four types of reels mentioned above.

fly reel —

closed-face reel

multiplying reel —

spinning reel

SETTING THE DRAG

One of the most important jobs of the reel is to provide the right amount of resistance, or drag, when playing, or reeling in, a fish. The drag should be set so that a fish can pull some line out when it is fighting hard, but it should require the fish to use some force. All reels have a knob or lever to adjust drag. To set the drag

on a spinning or closed-face reel, hold the rod in one hand and pull on the line with the other. The rod should bend a little bit before the line starts coming off the reel.

TACKLING THE TACKLE BOX

Many people think that supplying and organizing your **tackle** box is one of the most enjoyable parts of fishing. Choose a tackle box that is the right size for your fishing style. It should have different-sized compartments to keep your tackle neat and organized so you can easily find whatever you want.

Here are some of the most important items in a well-stocked tackle box:

TACKLE BOX SUPPLIES

Hooks. Anglers lose a lot of hooks. They get snagged on weeds, rocks, and other underwater objects. Hooked fish sometimes cut the line with their teeth or break it by pulling hard on it. There will also be times that you will want to change from a larger to a smaller hook, or the other way around.

Floats. Floats are round or **oblong** shapes made of plastic that are attached to a line a certain distance above the bait. They float at the surface of the water, and their movement shows when a fish has taken the bait. Floats come in all shapes and sizes depending on the type of water to be fished. Stock your tackle box with a variety.

Lures. **Lures** are artificial baits, and they come in a wide variety of shapes, sizes, materials, and colours. To get started, pick lures that are the right size for your rod and reel. If you really catch the fishing fever, you will probably make regular additions to your collection of lures.

Weights. Weights are used to drag your bait to the depth of the water where the fish are. Some weights are attached to the line with a hole, or eye. Others have a slit that can be pinched around the line (called slit shot). It is a good idea to have a mix of different weights, shapes, and sizes.

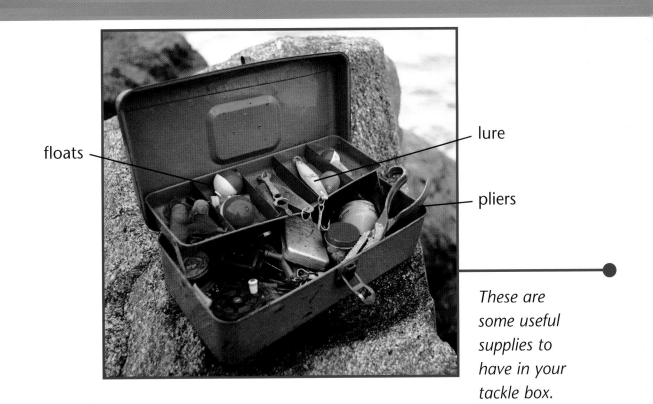

floats

lure

pliers

These are some useful supplies to have in your tackle box.

Here are some other useful angling supplies:

OTHER ANGLING SUPPLIES

Needle-nosed pliers come in handy to bend hooks back into shape and to get hooks out of a fish's mouth.

A disgorger is used for extracting hooks that are deep in a fish's mouth.

Sunblock is important to protect your skin from the sun's rays when outdoors, especially your face and hands.

A small *file* is useful for sharpening dull hooks.

A small *scale* and *ruler* will allow you to weigh and measure the fish you catch.

Polarized sunglasses are specially designed to filter out **glare** and allow you to see fish and other objects under the water. It is always important to use sunglasses to protect your eyes from bright sunlight.

CHOOSING YOUR BAIT

Choosing the right bait is a very important part of successful fishing. The first thing to consider when choosing bait is whether to use live or artificial bait.

LIVE BAIT

Live bait is the real food that fish eat, and fish are very willing to bite it. Live bait includes small fish such as roach, minnows, gudgeon, and small trout. Anglers often use maggots, worms, and insects as live bait.

Live bait like this is guaranteed to attract fish.

roach

minnow

worms

ARTIFICIAL BAIT

The many types of artificial bait, or **lures,** are designed to attract a fish's attention or to fool it into thinking a lure is food, or both. Some lures look a lot like live bait. Others are just brightly coloured, or have flashy moving parts. Some of them make noise as they move through the water.

DECIDING WHICH BAIT TO USE

A beginning angler might want to choose live bait over artificial because it is easier to catch fish with live bait. But artificial bait is more convenient to use. You do not have to worry about keeping it alive, as you do with live bait. You can keep it in your **tackle** box. As long as you do not lose it, you can use it over and over again.

In sunny, clear water, light-coloured lures are usually better than darker ones. The opposite is true for dark, cloudy water. Another way to choose bait is to "match the hatch". This expression refers to the fact that fish eat **prey** that is available. When there are a lot of minnows available, they eat minnows. When certain kinds of insects hatch, such as mayflies, fish will be looking for mayflies. If you offer bait or lures that look like the type of prey the fish are eating, you will be more likely to catch fish.

LURES AND FLIES

Artificial bait includes spinners, plugs, jigs, soft plastics, spoons, and flies. Spinners have shiny metal blades that spin around as you retrieve them. Most plugs are made of plastic. They usually have two or more three-pronged hooks called treble hooks hanging from them. Jigs are simple lures made up of a hook with a lead weight moulded around it. Soft plastics are rubbery and are designed to look and feel like live bait. Spoons are curved, blade-shaped lures that flash in the water. Most spoons are made of metal that is shiny on one side and brightly painted on the other. Most flies look like various types of insects. They are made by tying bits of hair, fur, or feathers onto a hook.

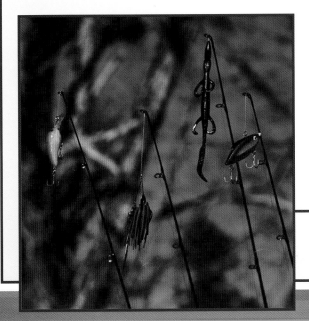

This picture shows a variety of lures.

Before you can start fishing, you will need to set up your **rig.** Each rig has the same basic parts, but may have a different kind of rod, reel, and bait set-up. Here is how to set up a float rig with a worm as bait.

ASSEMBLING THE ROD AND REEL

If your rod has two or three sections, you have to put it together. Hold the handle and gently slide the next section into the hole at the end of the handle section. Make sure the guides are lined up. Do the same with the third section, if there is one.

Now attach the reel. A spinning reel goes on the bottom side of the rod handle. Slide the reel's foot into the slot on the handle, called the reel seat. Slide the locking ring over the upper part of the reel foot and screw it on snugly.

TYING ON THE TACKLE

Pull some line from the reel and thread it through the circular guides on the rod. Slide the float onto the line, and using pliers, attach the split shot to hold the float in place. Then tie on the hook – use one of the angler's knots shown on the next page. Add more split shot near the hook to sink the bait.

There are several ways to attach a worm to a hook. You may hook the worm through the very end so that it moves freely in the water. Or you may slide the hook through the worm to hide the hook completely. You may also hook the worm several times to bunch it up.

BASIC ANGLER'S KNOTS

You can use these simple knots to attach a hook or **lure** to your line. When tying any knot, wet the line with water to make it slippery. Always trim the excess line with scissors close to the knot.

Trilene knot
1. Thread the line through the hook's eye twice to form a double loop.
2. Working upwards from the loop, wrap the end of the line around the main line four or five times.
3. Thread the end of the line back through the double loop and pull tight.

Improved clinch knot
1. Pull about 15 centimetres (6 inches) of line through the hook's eye.
2. Hold the end of the line against the main line and twist the hook around six times.
3. Thread the end of the line through the loop near the hook and then back through the loop above it.
4. Hold the end of the line and the main line and pull them snugly against the eye of the hook.

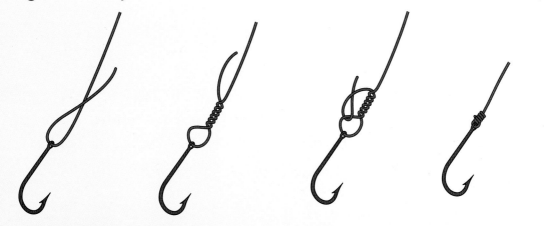

CASTING

The easiest way to cast is simply by throwing your line into the water. As you become a more experienced angler, you may want to learn various techniques for casting with different rods and reels. But as a beginner, you can start by learning two basic casts with a spinning reel.

A good way to remember the correct movements for casting is to picture a clock face. The important positions are 10 o'clock and 2 o'clock.

THE OVERHEAD CAST

Picture yourself standing directly in front of a giant clock, with your side to the clock face. Above your head is the 12 o'clock position.

1 Open the **bail arm** on the reel, and hook your index finger around the line.

2 Bring the rod back over your shoulder to point to where the 2 would be on the clock (if you are right-handed) or where the 10 would be on the clock (if you are left-handed). Look at the photo on the left for a demonstration of how to do this.

3 Pitch the rod forwards smoothly. When your rod gets to about the 10 o'clock position (for right-handers) or the 2 o'clock position (for left-handers), remove your index finger from the line. See photo on the right for an example.

THE SIDEARM CAST

Picture yourself standing in the middle of a clock face, with your casting arm at 12 o'clock. Your head would be pointing to the 3 on the clock.

1 Open the bail arm on the reel. Hook your index finger around the line.

2 Bring the rod back behind you to about the 2 o'clock position if you are right-handed or the 10 o'clock position if you are left-handed.

3 Pitch the rod forwards smoothly. When your rod gets to about the 10 o'clock position (for right-handers) or the 2 o'clock position (for left-handers), remove your index finger from the line.

FLY CASTING

Fly casting uses a special type of rod, reel, line, and **lures** called flies. The angler **retrieves** the fly in a technique called stripping, in which he or she pulls directly on the line with the fingers. Fish often strike during stripping.

FINDING FISH

The two most important keys to successful fishing are knowing where the fish are and what the fish want. To work out these things, experienced anglers look at a number of conditions such as weather, season, water temperature, the kind of fish they are fishing for, and the natural food available to the fish.

This smallmouth bass, found in the USA, is looking for other fish to feed on around these underwater rocks.

One of the first things to know about fish is that they like **structures.** A structure is any type of underwater object that provides a good place for fish to hide and eat. A structure could be the hull of a sunken boat; a pile of logs, dead trees, or rocks; a weed bed; a dock or pier; or anything else that makes fish feel safe and secure. If you can find a structure, you will probably find fish.

MORE WAYS TO FIND FISH

Another way to find fish is to watch for signs of the fish themselves. Ripples on the surface of the water, a large splash, or a disturbance of smaller fish, or bait fish, can all be signs that a big fish is active nearby. Also pay attention to fish-eating water birds, such as herons, egrets, pelicans, and terns. Such birds often gather to feed on schools, or groups, of bait fish. Bigger fish do the same thing. So follow the birds to the bait fish and you might catch some fish.

POPULAR FRESHWATER FISH

	Name	Average length or weight	What is special about this fish?
	Barbel	1.4 to 3.6 kg (3 to 8 lbs)	strong against river flow; have a crescent-shaped mouth
	Common carp	35 to 100 cms (14 to 39 inches)	grow large in lakes but remain tiny in ponds
	Chub	7 to 8 kilograms (15 to 18 lbs)	likes running water under trees to catch insects, and worms
	Perch	500 to 900 grams (1 to 2 lbs)	common in the British Isles
	Pike	0.9 to 4.5 kilograms (2 to 10 lbs)	fierce **predator**; great fighter
	Rainbow trout	1 to 3.6 kg (2 to 8 lbs)	spectacular leaps when hooked
	Roach	285 to 680 gms (10 ounces to (1lb 8 ounces)	most popular fish with UK anglers
	Silver Bream	20 to 25 cms (8 to 10 inches)	nick-named "tin plate" because of its silver colour

The first step in catching a fish is getting a bite. You will know when you have a bite if you sense something alive on the end of your rod. Your rod tip might jerk lightly a few times. It may slowly bend with a kind of heavy feeling. Sometimes fish strike, or bite aggressively and hard. After a strike, the fish may "run" and the line may start spinning off the reel as the fish tries to swim away quickly.

SETTING THE HOOK AND PLAYING THE FISH

Now is the time to act fast and set the hook. You do this by quickly snapping up the tip of the rod to drive the hook into the fish's lip. Once you know the fish is hooked, keep steady pressure on the line as you reel in. If you let the line go limp, you give the fish a chance to spit out the hook or shake it out of its mouth. Raise the rod tip up to pull the fish towards you. Then lower it and reel only when there is slack in the line. If the fish starts swimming away, let it run. When it stops, once again pull the fish towards you, drop the rod tip, and reel in the slack. Repeat these actions until the fish is close to the bank or boat.

Be very careful when you are fishing on slippery surfaces, such as rocks that are near water.

LANDING THE FISH

Small fish can be **landed** by simply lifting them into the boat or on to the bank. You might need help to land a larger fish. Hold the rod upright and keep the fish close to the boat or bank and near the surface. A friend can then scoop the fish up in a net to avoid harming it. Experienced anglers sometimes land fish that do not have true teeth, by grabbing the bottom jaw with the thumb inside the mouth and the rest of the fingers cupping the **gill plate**.

Always make sure your hand is wet when you pick up a fish to avoid removing the fish's protective layer of slime. Fins and gill plates can be sharp, so watch out.

CATCH AND RELEASE

Many fishers practise catch-and-release angling. To make sure the fish is returned to the water unharmed, remember these points:

● Handle the fish as little as possible. Remove the hook quickly and gently, with a disgorger if necessary. If the hook is too deeply embedded in the fish's mouth, cut the line and leave the hook in. The hook will eventually dissolve.

● If you want to take a picture, have the camera ready before you take the fish from the water.

● Do not release the fish until it has recovered from being caught. Swish it gently back and forth under the water. The fish is ready to be released when its gill movements are strong and regular and when it can stay upright in the water.

Every angler over the age of 12 must have a special licence to fish for salmon, trout, freshwater fish or eels in England and Wales. This is called an Environment Agency Rod Fishing Licence. These licences are legal requirements which means that each angler must have one. You can buy them from Post Offices. Keep your licence with you when you are fishing.

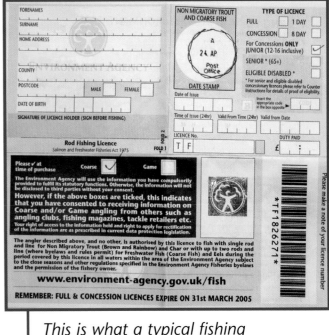

This is what a typical fishing licence looks like.

Only members of this angling club can fish here.

As well as a rod licence, you may need a permit. This is also known as a ticket or day ticket. A permit gives you permission to fish from a particular water that may belong to an angling club or fishery. Some waters are free, but it is important to check before you start fishing.

KEEPING FISH HEALTHY

Many rules are intended to keep the fish populations healthy. There are often **regulations** about when fishing is allowed. For instance, in many places you cannot fish for certain **species** of fish when they are **spawning.** Most fish are active and easy to catch during spawning. If they are caught before they have a chance to lay their eggs, a whole generation of new fish is lost. These rules protect the fish and allow them to **reproduce.**

As well as licences and permits, there are other rules for anglers. Some rules restrict the number and size of fish each angler can keep. For example, you may be allowed to take home only 2, 6, 10, or 20 of certain types of fish. Other regulations mean that you may have to release any fish that is smaller than a certain size limit. In a lot of club waters all fish have to be returned to the water alive. Check with the club, fishery, or organization that owns the waters, before you start fishing.

Many anglers begin fishing at a very young age like this boy.

FISHING SAFETY

Fishing is a fun, exciting sport. Following a few simple rules makes it a safe one, too.

- Never fish alone. It's best to fish with a responsible adult.

- Be careful when handling hooks. They are sharp.

- Look around and behind you before casting to make sure you do not snag anyone.

- Use care when handling fish. Some have sharp teeth, fins, and gill covers that can cause bad cuts.

- Protect your eyes and face from the sun and **glare** from the water by wearing a hat and sunglasses. Do not forget to use sunscreen, too.

It is a great feeling to be able to go out into nature and get your own food. Fish are also nutritious and delicious. They are low in fat and high in protein. They also contain substances called fatty acids, which help keep your **nervous system** healthy.

IS EATING FISH HARMFUL?

Some caution is needed when eating fish. Substances such as mercury and other chemicals sometimes get into the bodies of some fish in water. This can be harmful if a person eats too many of a certain type of fish. As a result, some health experts suggest that people limit the amount of certain **species** of fish that they eat. However, in the UK, most people only eat salmon and trout that they have caught. There is not usually so much pollution where these fish are found.

Anglers must learn how to clean and prepare a fish for cooking.

Many anglers enjoy cooking the fish they catch over an open fire. Remember to take all your litter home with you!

Boiling, sautéing, deep-frying, pan frying, grilling, smoking, and baking are some of the most popular ways to prepare fish. Fish is also delicious in stir-fries and soups.

PAN-FRIED FISH COATING

Pan frying is a popular way to prepare fish, and most anglers have their own favourite recipes for fish coating, which is also known as breading. Here is a recipe that you can try yourself.

$\frac{1}{2}$ cup (110 grams) cornmeal
1 cup (230 grams) flour
1 teaspoon salt
$\frac{1}{2}$ teaspoon pepper
2 teaspoon paprika
1 teaspoon garlic powder
1 teaspoon poultry seasoning or other herb mixture
Four fish fillets about 2.5 centimetres (1 inch) thick
Oil for frying

Mix the first seven ingredients on a piece of wax paper. One at a time, place a fish fillet in the coating mixture. Turn and pat each fillet so that they are well coated.

Pour oil into a steep-sided frying pan to a depth of about $\frac{1}{2}$ inch (1.3 centimetres). Ask an adult to heat the oil on medium heat until it is hot. The oil is at the right temperature when a little bit of coating mixture sizzles when dropped in the oil.

Ask an adult to place the fish in the oil. Cook the fillets about six minutes on each side. Adjust the cooking time for larger or smaller fillets.

Drain the fillets on paper towels before serving.

You might not think of fishing as a competitive sport, but it is. Every year there are hundreds of fishing tournaments, including **professional** matches for big-money prizes. Matches for **amateurs** are sponsored by fishing clubs and other organizations. Some amateur matches and competitions are just for fun. Others provide a way for serious anglers to work their way up to professional competitive events.

There are many different matches and events from the National Pike Angling Championships to the Junior International Championships. Depending on the event, the winner may be the angler who catches the largest fish or the most fish according to weight in a certain amount of time.

This 35-kilogram (77-pound) amberjack fish was caught at a tournament in Georgia, USA, in 1996.

JUNIOR MATCHES

In the UK, clubs organize local and regional and club matches for young anglers. In addition, the National Junior Angling Association hosts national competitions all over the country. The largest fishing programme in the world for children is the Kids All-American Fishing Derby, which consists of about 1800 separate competitions all over America for childen aged five to sixteen.

BRITISH RECORD FRESHWATER FISH

Type of fish	Weight	Place caught	Year
Barbel	8.8 kg (19 pounds 6 ounces)	Great Ouse River, Bedfordshire	2001
Bleak	129 grams (4 ounces)	River Lark, Cambridgeshire	1998
Bream (silver)	793 grams (1 pound 12 ounces)	Mill Farm Fishery, West Sussex	2003
Carp (mirror)	27.8 kg (61 pounds 7 ounces)	Conningbrook Lake, Kent	2002
Chub	3.9 kg (8 pounds 13 ounces)	Private Stillwater	2004
Dace	599 grams (1 pound 5 ounces)	River Weir	2002
Eel	5 kg (11 pounds 2 ounces)	Kingfisher Lake, Hampshire	1978
Perch	2.5 kg (5 pounds 9 ounces)	Glebe Lake, Fringford	2002
Pike	21.2 kg (46 pounds 13 ounces)	Llandegfedd, Wales	1992
Roach	1.8 kg (4 pounds 3 ounces)	River Stour, Dorset	1990
Rudd	2.1 kg (4 pounds 10 ounces)	Freshwater Lake, Northern Ireland	2001
Salmon (Atlantic)	29 kg (64 pounds)	River Tay, Scotland	1922
Trout (brown, natural)	14.4 kg (31 pounds 12 ounces)	Lock Awe, Argyll, Scotland	2002

Anywhere there is a body of water, you will probably find anglers. With the widespread availability of fishing **tackle**, freshwater sport fishing is similar throughout the world. What is different are the types of fish anglers catch.

Sport anglers in India cast their lines into the rivers hoping to catch the majestic golden mahseer. This fish regularly grows up to 31.8 kilograms (70 pounds) and can reach 56.7 kilograms (125 pounds).

The Amazon River has an incredible number of amazing sport fish. One of the most popular and beautiful is the peacock bass. These fish can grow to well over 9.1 kilograms (20 pounds). Anglers catch them in quiet **lagoons** that are attached to the river. Peacock bass are not true bass, such as the largemouth and smallmouth bass of North America. Instead, they are part of a family of tropical freshwater fish called cichlids.

Mahseer, found in India, can grow to be very large. Their lips are good for eating things from the bottoms of lakes and rivers.

OTHER AMAZON FISH

Other giant Amazon fish are the arapaima and the payara. The arapaima has to breathe air at the surface. The payara is a fearsome **predator** with long, razor-sharp teeth in its lower jaw. This fish's strength and fighting ability provide a thrilling experience for anglers.

The taimen is a large fish of eastern Asia. These fish are believed to be a more ancient form of the salmon and trout of North America. In the rivers of Siberia, taimen can reach huge sizes. The largest recorded taimen weighed in at almost 113.4 kilograms (250 pounds).

In Asia and tropical Africa, one of the most popular game fish is the hard-fighting snakehead. These fish have tasty flesh and grow up to 1 metre (3 feet) in length.

TALE OF A TAIMEN

According to a Mongolian folktale, a group of lost and starving tribesmen found a giant taimen frozen in the ice. They survived all winter long by cutting pieces of flesh from the fish. When the ice began to melt in the spring, the tribesmen were astonished to see the great fish wiggle free from the ice and swim away!

These snakehead fish were photographed using their fins to move along the ground. Snakehead fish have been found in the USA and could threaten local fish populations.

UNWELCOME SETTLERS

The snakehead made news in the USA in 2002 when two adult snakeheads and about 100 of their young were discovered in a Maryland lake. Wildlife officials established that the two adult fish came from an Asian food market. Snakeheads have also been found in lakes and ponds in several other states. Wildlife officials fear that if the population of these fish-gobbling predators grows, it may threaten many **species** of **native** fish.

GLOSSARY

amateur   person who does something for enjoyment rather than for money

archaeologist   scientist who learns about ancient people by studying their tools, buildings, and utensils

bail arm   part of a reel that either allows or prevents line coming off the spool

fibreglass   glass in the form of very fine threads. Fiberglass is blended with plastic to make fishing rods.

gill plate   flap of bone that covers a fish's gill

glare   harsh, brilliant light

graphite   soft, black mineral that is used to make fishing rods

lagoon   small, shallow pond connected to a larger body of water

land   to catch a fish

lure   artificial bait used for catching fish

native   living or growing in nature in a particular area or region

nervous system   bodily system that sends nerve impulses to organs that make actions. In humans, the nervous system includes the brain, spinal cord, and nerves around the body.

oblong   shape that is longer in one direction than the other

predator   animal that kills and eats other animals in order to live

prey   animal that is hunted or killed by other animals for food

professional   person who does something for money rather than just for enjoyment

regulation   rule that explains the way something should be done

reproduce   produce new individuals, or offspring, of the same kind

retrieve   to reel in a lure

rig   rod, reel, and bait or lure that are set up and used for angling

spawn   to produce new young, sometimes by laying and fertilizing eggs

species   category of living, related things that are able to produce offspring

structure   any type of underwater object that provides a good place for fish to hide and eat

synthetic   not existing naturally; man-made

tackle   all the equipment used for angling

MORE BOOKS TO READ

Faxfinder: Fishing by Chris Bell (Collins, 1996)

Funfax: Beginners Guide to Fishing by Steve Gilbert (Dorling Kindersley, 1992)

Go for Sport!: Fishing by Gareth Parnell, Alan Barnes and Peter Maskell (Hodder Children's Books, 1993)

Start Fishing! by L. Sims (Usborne Books, 2005)

TAKING IT FURTHER

Angling UK
www.anglinguk.net/sitemap.htm

British Disabled Angling Association
www.bdaa.co.uk

British Record (rod-caught) Fish Committee
www.nfsa.org.uk/ntcg/brfc/record_list_coarse_fish.htm

Environment Agency
www.environmentagency.gov.uk/fish

National Federation of Anglers
www.nfadirect.com/home.php

National Junior Angling Association
www.nja.org/uk

Pike Anglers Club of Great Britain
www.pacgb.com

Salmon and Trout Association
www.salmon-trout.org.uk

www.maggotdrowning.com
fishing information on fisheries, tackle shops, etc.

www.ansa.com.au
website for the Australian National Sportfishing Association.

Titles in the *Get Going: Hobbies* series include:

Hardback   0 431 11050 6

Hardback   0 431 11051 4

Hardback   0 431 11052 2

Find out about the other titles in this series on our website www.heinemann.co.uk/library